MORE Keep 'em Reading BULLETIN BOARDS

Year-round Designs for the Library and Classroom

Illustrated by Stan Jusan

Fort Atkinson, Wisconsin

Published by UpstartBooks
W5527 Highway 106
P.O. Box 800
Fort Atkinson, Wisconsin 53538-0800
1-800-448-4887

Cover design: Heidi Green, illustrations by Stan Tusan

The paper used in this publication meets the minimum requirements of American National Standard for Information Science — Permanence of Paper for Printed Library Material. ANSI/NISO Z39.48-1992.

Contents

Introduction

More Keep 'em Reading Bulletin Boards offers more of the same great reading-promotional bulletin board ideas as the first book, as well as some fun, new themes. All of the bulletin boards are created especially for the library media center and include themes to use everyday, seasonally and for special occasions. Each bulletin board features characters reading or holding books.

The book is divided into three main sections—seasons, holidays and special events and all-occasion boards—for easy reference.

Each bulletin board theme includes:

- a choice of reading and book-related slogans
- an illustration of a suggested design
- large and small bold, clean-lined patterns for easy copying and tracing
- decoration and display suggestions
- additional thematic ideas

Creating Your Bulletin Boards

Each bulletin board pattern includes individual pieces to allow you to mix and match to meet your design and decoration needs. We suggest one way of putting the pieces together, but we encourage you to use your imagination!

The most popular configuration is a main piece surrounded by smaller pieces featuring the names of each student who has completed the reading list or some other goal (see illustration below). This simple design saves you time and makes your board easy to read and understand.

To enlarge the patterns for tracing, use an opaque or overhead projector and transparency copies of the patterns. Trace onto large sheets or rolls of paper. To save time—and your hand—try stacking and cutting out like pieces.

We hope you'll find that the patterns, slogans and decoration suggestions are just a springboard for your own creative ideas and displays.

Preserving Your Bulletin Boards

To use your bulletin board pieces again and again, laminate the individual pieces or laminate whole bulletin boards together. Then store the pieces flat in drawers or shelves. Label the storage with the name or theme of the bulletin board so it is easy to locate at a later date.

If you choose to disassemble your board but want to recreate it at another time, take a photo of the completed board to help you put it back together quickly and accurately.

Getting Kids Involved

Children love projects, and they love to be helpers. Give them the opportunity to do both by having them help assemble your bulletin boards. This could include tracing the patterns, creating backgrounds, cutting out pieces or making their own pieces for display.

Special Touches

In addition to the uniqueness children's creations will lend your bulletin boards, you may also consider the following enhancements:

- use fabric, specialty papers, corrugated paper and other materials to make interesting backgrounds and borders
- treat papers and fabrics to create unique looks, including crinkling, folding, dying and weaving
- create three-dimensional bulletin board pieces by gluing or sewing pieces together and stuffing them with cotton batting or tissue

- use craft materials to create special effects: glitter and glitter glue, raffia, ribbon, coated wires, etc.
- create borders to cover up uneven background edges
- use paint as a substitute for drawing, or to create a special texture or look

Table Displays

For an easy way to tie books and other materials to the theme, place a table in front of your bulletin board and collect items from the school and/or community to enrich the display.

Supply Sources

Party supply stores are great sources for decorations of all kinds, and paper outlet stores offer color and size choices your standard supplier might not. If your community has a textile, rubber, plastics or other materials manufacturing plant nearby, the scraps and seconds can make great crafting materials as well.

Fall

Design Suggestion

Alternative Themes

Harvest

Nature

Gophers

Alternative Slogans

The following slogans are suggestions that can be used with the various art pieces supplied.

1. Fall for Books
2. I'm Nuts About Books
3. Leaf through a Good Book
4. Drop in and Read

Decoration and Display Suggestions

- Use the gopher or a paper tree as the main focus. Then write students' names and books read on paper leaves and have them "fall."
- Write students' names and books read on paper pumpkins or acorns.
- Create a border with real leaves or hang real leaves from the ceiling.
- Have students collect real leaves to display. Help them identify the trees they came from, then label the leaves and attach them to the board.
- Set up a table display with fall books. Add pumpkins, squash, corn-husks and other fall vegetables.

Winter

Design Suggestion

Alternative Themes

Holidays

Winter Outdoor Fun

Alternative Slogans

The following slogans are suggestions that can be used with the various art pieces supplied.

1. Books Are Cool
2. Snow is Falling—Books Are Calling
3. Scarf Up a Good Book!
4. Skate Into Reading

Decoration and Display Suggestions

- Write students' names and books read on mugs of hot cocoa. Post them on the board.
- With the snowmen, use a permanent marker to label Styrofoam snowballs with students' names and books read. Hang from the ceiling.
- Have students cut out snowflakes and label them with their names and books read. Post them on the board. Hang paper icicles around area.
- Host a mitten/scarf drive for underprivileged children. Before donating, use donations as decorations for the scarf slogan.
- Use cotton batting for snow, blue cellophane for an ice skating pond and styrofoam balls for snowballs.

Read

Design Suggestion

Alternative Themes

Gardening

Bugs

Rainy Days

Flowers

Alternative Slogans

The following slogans are suggestions that can be used with the various art pieces supplied.

1. Bloom with Books!
2. Don't Bug Me—I'm Reading
3. Shower Yourself with Books
4. The Buzz is ... Reading!
5. Spring into Reading

Decoration and Display Suggestions

- Set up a table display with toy gardening tools and books in a wheelbarrow. Or fill terra cotta pots with fake flowers and books.
- Write students' names and books read on the book the bug is reading. Post around board.
- Use the "Plant Yourself" slogan and put each student's picture in the center of the small flower illustration. Display on the board.
- Cut raindrops out of construction paper and write students' names and books read on each one. Post with bug under umbrella.
- Have students create new book titles relating to plants. Display them on the board.

Summer

Design Suggestion

Alternative Themes

Vacation

Ocean

Alternative Slogans

The following slogans are suggestions that can be used with the various art pieces supplied.

1. Stay Cool ... Read!
2. Surf's Up! Read!
3. Fun in the Sun—Read!
4. Dive into a Good Book
5. Make Waves—Read!

Decoration and Display Suggestions

- Use sandpaper to create a beach, and rippled blue cellophane or plastic wrap for water.
- Create a table display in front with children's flotation devices and pail and shovel sets filled with books about summer activities.
- Have students color in their own pail, then label them with their name and books read. Post them on the board.
- Write titles of summer activity books on the sun. Post them on the board. Set up a table display of the books.
- Set up a beach retreat with a lounge chair, umbrella and beach towel. Play a tape of ocean sounds.

Design Suggestion

Alternative Theme

Scary Stories

Alternative Slogans

The following slogans are suggestions that can be used with the various art pieces supplied.

1. Scare Up a Good Book
2. Ghoulishly Good Tales
3. Spin a Spooky Tale
4. It's No Trick ... Books are Treats!
5. Dr. Franken-Read
6. Monster Readers

Decoration and Display Suggestions

- Drape white sheets along the edge of the bulletin board to create ghost-like images. As students finish reading books, write each title on an open book and post.
- Cut a ghost shape out of an old white sheet and display on the board.
- Have each student make a pumpkin face and write a favorite book on it. Display on the board.
- Set up a table display with a trick-or-treat bag full of candy, carved jack-o'-lanterns and scary stories.
- Use black paper for the background and create a border with plastic spiders.

BOO

Design Suggestion

Alternative Theme

General Reading

Alternative Slogans

The following slogans are suggestions that can be used with the various art pieces supplied.

1. Every Day is a Great Day to Read
2. Celebrate Books!
3. Catch a Good Book
4. Be a Weekly Reader
5. Get Into a Good Book

Decoration and Display Suggestions

- Write students' names and books read on the open book. Display them around the board.
- Set up a display of favorite authors and illustrators. Read a story from one author each day.
- Set up a table with mini-displays of books by genre. If possible, use props such as a football or baseball with books about sports, and stuffed animals with books about animals.
- Have students draw a character or scene from their favorite book. Display around the board.
- Ask older students to choose a day of the week and a book to read. Have them write their name and book on the calendar, then read the story to a younger class on the designated day.

I
READ!

SUN
MON
TUE
WED
THURS
FRI
SAT

Thanksgiving

Design Suggestion

Alternative Themes

Fall

Harvest

Alternative Slogans

The following slogans are suggestions that can be used with the various art pieces supplied.

1. Gobble up a Good Book!
2. Happy Thanksreading
3. Don't be a Turkey—Read!
4. Harvest a Good Book

Decoration and Display Suggestions

- Write students' names and books read on the leaves. Display them around the board.
- Set up a table display with a cornucopia spilling over with fall vegetables, corn-husk dolls and related books.
- Make a border out of real feathers and leaves. Feathers are available at craft stores.
- Have students write acrostics for the word "Thanksgiving." Post the poems on the board.
- Have students write a list or paragraph about what they are thankful for. Post responses on the board.

Design Suggestion

Alternative Theme

Winter

Alternative Slogans

The following slogans are suggestions that can be used with the various art pieces supplied.

1. Season's Readings
2. Rudolph the Reading Reindeer
3. 'Tis the Season for Books and Reading
4. Wrap up a Good Book!

Decoration and Display Suggestions

- Borrow nutcrackers from friends in your school and community. Set up a table display with the nutcrackers and holiday books.
- Cut out paper nuts. Have students write their names and books read on the nuts. Display them around the board.
- Have students cut out snowflakes for the border. Use cotton batting for snow.
- Use wrapping paper and ribbons as your background and border. Write students' names and books read on the presents. Display them around the board.
- Make a border with holiday lights or a red and green paper chain.

Chinese New Year

Design Suggestion

Alternative Themes

China

Celebrations Around the World

Alternative Slogans

The following slogans are suggestions that can be used with the various art pieces supplied.

1. Happy Chinese New Year!
2. Ring in the New Year with Books
3. Celebrate the Year of the Book
4. Quit Drag-on—Read!

Decoration and Display Suggestions

- Cut out images of the 12 animals in the Chinese zodiac. Display on the board. Include the characteristics of each zodiac sign.
- Make lanterns by folding a piece of paper in half the long way and cutting 18 3½" slits. Unfold the paper and glue the short ends together. Hang the lanterns from the ceiling.
- Set up a table display with books about Chinese New Year. Set out tangerines, oranges, plum blossoms and water narcissus—all symbols of the Chinese New Year.
- Have students write their wishes for the new year. Post them on the board.

Valentine's Day

Design Suggestion

Alternative Themes

Book Lovers

General Reading

Library Birthday

Alternative Slogans

The following slogans are suggestions that can be used with the various art pieces supplied.

1. Books Warm the Heart!
2. Books Are My Valentine!
3. Share a Book with Someone You Love
4. Reading is Close to My Heart

Decoration and Display Suggestions

- Make the background with red, white or pink paper, or use all three colors. Create a border using lace or paper doilies.
- Have students come up with new candy heart slogans relating to books and reading. Post them on hearts on the board.
- Write students' names and books read on the hearts. Display them on the board.
- Make a border using candy hearts.
- Set up a table display featuring books with Valentine's Day and love themes.

National Library Week

Design Suggestion

Alternative Themes

Library Birthday

General Reading

Alternative Slogans

The following slogans are suggestions that can be used with the various art pieces supplied.

1. Celebrate with Books!
2. Launch Your Imagination—Read!
3. Run Away and Read
4. Liftoff with a Library Card

Decoration and Display Suggestions

- Have students design their own library card. They can include their name and a favorite book. Post them on the board.
- Write students' names and books read on the book with snake. Display around the board.
- Set up a display of new books. Post descriptions of the books on the board. Have students try to match the description to the title.
- Have students write their favorite thing about the library on the book with snake. Post them around the board.
- Have students write poems about the library. Display them on the board.

LIBRARY
CARD

Cats

Design Suggestion

Alternative Theme

Pets

Alternative Slogans

The following slogans are suggestions that can be used with the various art pieces supplied.

1. Books Make Me Purr
2. Books Are Purr-fect
3. Books Are the Cats' Meow
4. Sink Your Claws into a Good Book

Decoration and Display Suggestions

- Write students' names and books read on the reading cat. Display them on the board.
- Set up a display of books about cats. Include relevant props such as plush cats or cat toys.
- Ask students to bring in pictures of their cats. Have them write a few sentences about their cats. Post the pictures and descriptions around the board.
- Display the names of favorite literary cats on the board. Set up a display of the books.
- Cut out a cat for each student. Have the students decorate the cats. Then have them write their names and favorite cat books on the cats. Post them on the board.

Dogs

Design Suggestion

Alternative Theme

Pets

Alternative Slogans

The following slogans are suggestions that can be used with the various art pieces supplied.

1. Books Are Man's Best Friend
2. Books Are Dog-gone Good
3. Rub My Tummy—Read!
4. Unleash Your Mind—Read
5. Bark for Books!

Decoration and Display Suggestions

- Write students' names and books read on the dog dish. Display them around the board.
- Ask students to bring in pictures of their dogs. Have them write a few sentences about their dogs. Post the pictures and descriptions on the board.
- Set up a table display of books about dogs. Include relevant props such as dog bones or plush dogs.
- Cut out dog bones. Use them for a border or write students' names and books read on them.
- Use dog leashes as a border. Cut out dog tags for each student. Have the students write their name and favorite dog book on the tag.

Design Suggestion

Alternative Themes

Nature

Rain Forest

Alternative Slogans

The following slogans are suggestions that can be used with the various art pieces supplied.

1. Pig Out on Books
2. Go on a Safa-Read
3. Reading Rain Forest
4. Books Are Great—I'm Not Lion

Decoration and Display Suggestions

- Set up a table display of the plant, animal and insect life in the jungle, including plastic and plush models and related books.
- Write students' names and books read on the book with vine. Display them on the board.
- Create a bamboo and leaf border. Write students' names and books read on leaves. Post them on the board.
- Cut plants, animals and insects out of fun foam. Add them to the bulletin board for a three-dimensional look.
- Have students draw and cut out their favorite jungle animal. Include a related book that they read on their animal.

Design Suggestion

Alternative Themes

Fantasy

Science Fiction

Travel

Alternative Slogans

The following slogans are suggestions that can be used with the various art pieces supplied.

1. Blast Off With a Good Book!
2. Rocket into Reading
3. Launch Your Imagination—Read!
4. Find Your Reading Space

Decoration and Display Suggestions

- Cut out star and planet shapes. Write students' names and books read in each shape. Display them on the board.
- Set up a table display with books about space, astronauts, etc.
- Get lids for slushies from a convenience store. Put a student's picture under each lid so it looks like they are in space ships. Have them write where they would go if they were an astronaut.
- Make rockets out of toilet paper tubes covered in aluminum foil. Add a top and tail to each rocket. Have students write their names and favorite outer space book on their rocket.

Patriotic

Design Suggestion

Alternative Themes

Fourth of July

Flag Day

Memorial Day

Alternative Slogans

The following slogans are suggestions that can be used with the various art pieces supplied.

1. Stars, Stripes and Books Forever!
2. Bring Four-th Books!
3. Star Spangled Reader
4. Salute to Books
5. Red, White and Books!

Decoration and Display Suggestions

- Make a background with red and white construction paper stripes.
- Make a border with red, white and blue crepe paper streamers.
- Have students create flags using strips of construction paper. Ask them to write an acrostic poem about flags using the word flag. Write each line on a stripe of the flag. Post the poems on the board.
- Cut out a star for each student. Have them write their names and a wish for the future. Post the stars around the board.
- Set up a table display of related stories and nonfiction books about our country.

Design Suggestion

Alternative Themes

Adventure

Vacation

Maps

Geography

Alternative Slogans

The following slogans are suggestions that can be used with the various art pieces supplied.

1. Soar With Books!
2. Map Your Future—Read!
3. Reading Road Trip
4. Take Off with Books
5. Travel the World with Books

Decoration and Display Suggestions

- Put up a large map of the United States. Each time a student reads a book based in the U.S., place a pushpin in the map at the book's location.
- Put up a large map of the United States. Put a pushpin at each place a student has visited.
- Write students' names and books read in the blank book. Post them on the board.
- Have students bring in a vacation photo and write about where they went. Display them on the board.
- Set up a table display of maps, globes and books about travel.

READ
READ

READ

Race Cars

Design Suggestion

Alternative Theme

Winning

Alternative Slogans

The following slogans are suggestions that can be used with the various art pieces supplied.

1. Take the Lead—Read!
2. Rev Up with Good Books
3. Speed into Reading
4. Join the Winner's Circle

Decoration and Display Suggestions

- Have a reading race. Make a race track with two or more cars on the bulletin board. Divide a class or grade into teams. As each team accomplishes a reading goal, move their car along the track. Give each member of the winning team a small checkered flag.
- Cut out a checkered flag for each student. Have them write their names and books read in the flag's squares. Post them on the board.
- Set up a table display with books about cars and racing. If possible, include a checkered flag, helmet and other props.
- Cut out a race car for each student. Write students' names and books read on each car. Display the cars around a track on the board.

3

READ

1ST

Camping

Design Suggestion

Alternative Themes

Summer Camp

Outdoors

Vacation

Alternative Slogans

The following slogans are suggestions that can be used with the various art pieces supplied.

1. Catch a Good Book
2. Can't See the Forest for the Reads
3. Discover New Trails
4. Pine for Books

Decoration and Display Suggestions

- Cut out a tent for each student. Have the students decorate their tents. Cut a slit up the middle of each tent for the opening. Post them on the board with the students' pictures in the tent openings.
- Set up a table display with camping equipment and books about camping. Set out a backpack and have it overflowing with books.
- Have students write their names and books read on the leaves. Post them on the board.
- Make a border with leaves and twigs.
- Use yellow and red cellophane or tissue paper and construction paper logs to make a campfire. Display spooky campfire stories.

READ
READ

READ